OVERCOMING PREJUDICE

In The Church

BY

PASTOR DENNIS LEONARD

> This book is dedicated with love to the congregation of Heritage Christian Center. Their willingness to reach out in love to this lost and dying world according to God's Word, is a testimony that prejudice and hate can be overcome with the love of Jesus Christ.
>
> **Pastor Dennis Leonard**

All rights reserved.
Dennis Leonard Publications

Copyright © 1993
Dennis Leonard Publications
1301 South Clinton Street
Denver, Colorado 80231
(303) 369-8514

Contents

1. Prejudice In The Church 9

2. Overcoming Hatred 17

3. We Are All The Same In Christ 31

4. Enlarging Your Circle Of Love 37

5. Church Of All Nations 43

Introduction

"Unless the Lord builds the house, they labor in vain who build it." (Psalms 127:1)

God had placed a burden on my heart to preach the gospel to a lost and dying world. As I began to seek Him early in this ministry, He spoke these words to my heart. *"Build a church for all people no matter who they are, no matter what their social standing, no matter their color, race or denomination. I want you to build a church of all nations that stands for Jesus."*

I asked the Lord how my wife and I were going to appeal to people from all walks of life. I felt His answer rise up on the inside of me saying, *"Just preach Jesus and love everybody the same, because in Me there is no difference."*

My wife and I began to pray and believe God for the vision He had placed in our hearts. We grew from a small handful of people...to 20 people. Then the Lord impressed upon me to pray for the Black Community. Soon God brought a black piano player into our church, and then a black family. We could see God doing something in our midst. He began to move in our church and brought in people of all colors, races, and denominations.

In these last days, God is knitting the body of Christ together, to bring down the walls of prejudice. God is love, and He is pouring His love out on His people, teaching them that we are all one in Him.

God hates prejudice, and yet, every one of us to a certain extent has prejudice within us. Whether we are willing to admit it or face it, every single person alive has some form of prejudice somewhere in their life.

Prejudice begins with a spirit of fear that comes in when one person is suspicious or fearful of another group of people. Prejudice takes place when bitterness or hatred builds up because an individual did not forgive an incident or circumstance that happened in their life.

We must all guard against prejudice in our lives. Like so many other issues in our Christian walk, it comes down to a matter of choice. We must make a decision to turn the hurts and cares of this world over to the Lord, and choose to walk in love.

Prejudice will stop God's miracle for your life. This book examines prejudice in the church and what we as the body of Christ can do to overcome the resurgence of hate and fear that is evident not only in our society, but in our churches today.

God tells us in I Corinthians 11:31, *"If we will judge ourselves, we will not be judged."* God wants to resolve the issues of prejudice within you, right now. Are you willing to examine your heart and become everything God has called you to be? Ask yourself: To what extent am I prejudiced?

Chapter One
Prejudice in the Church

There was a time in America's history when black people were being lynched by the hundreds. The KKK was strong in our country and was spreading its rhetoric and lies. Black people were forced to sit in the back of white churches. They could not go forward for prayer or to spend time at the altar. The white man felt he was superior to the black race, and did not want the black man worshipping with him.

God caused a movement to overcome this at the turn of the century. This movement diabolically opposed the spiritual views held by society. In 1906, the power of God flowed forth at the Azuza Street Revival. People from all walks of life were drawn to Azuza Street to witness this great outpouring of God's love through the Holy Spirit. God anointed a black man, Pastor William Seymour, to deliver the message that racial prejudice was not for the body of Christ. This was the first time in history that people of all races came to listen to a black man preach. For a time, it looked as if the church was going to become integrated. After several years, people rejected that unity and segregation once again began in the body of Christ.

With all the KKK activity and open prejudice at

that time, you can see what a miracle God wrought at the Azuza Street Revival. People of different colors and races were worshipping together in one accord. The Holy Spirit crossed all color and racial barriers then and He'll lead you to do the same thing now.

Today, hatred between races is growing. Germany is experiencing a rebirth of the Nazi party. Yugoslavia is being ripped apart by racial strife and they call it "ethnic cleansing." Recently in Italy, they have decided that they don't want Jews in their country. Our world is sick and prejudice has become the disease of choice. This resurgence of hate and intolerance is not only found in the world, but also in the church. Anti-semetic doctrines are creeping into the churches that once taught only the gospel of Jesus Christ. Our spiritual enemy is doing everything he can to separate people. Certain religious movements in our country are calling for the separation of races. How can we evangelize our neighborhoods, let alone our world if we have prejudice within us? In Mark 3:25, Jesus said, "A house divided cannot stand." We are the body of Christ and the enemy wants to divide us and separate us with prejudice.

What Is Prejudice?

Prejudice is the act of prejudging a race of people because of the color of their skin or the way they look.

It is an irrational suspicion that can grow into the hatred of an entire group of people.

Prejudice is a spiritual battle perpetrated by the enemy. He plans strategies against people and he starts with children. He'll send somebody along that is of a different skin color to call a child names. He'll start with young children that are not able to detect his schemes, and through this experience they feel the pain of rejection. Weaknesses are then created, and the child begins to build walls in their life as a means of protection. Teenagers transfer their anger of rejection to one another and hostility begins to spread like a cancer. As adults, those weaknesses and hurts are displayed as prejudice.

Growing up in Christ is a life long process. Through this maturing process often there are attitudes and behaviors that God needs to take out of us...like prejudice.

You don't have to be white to be prejudiced. There are people who are prejudiced against their own race. Some black people won't date other black people and there are white people that won't date white people. Black people tell me they have a difficult time living with the effects of slavery. For hundreds of years these people were stripped of their unity, their family, and their dignity. They were told that they would never amount to anything. They were taught that the darker their skin, the less acceptable they were to society and their own people as well. Prejudice is not limited to one culture or one group of people, it affects us all. However, God has a training program for Christians. He desires for each of us to overcome prejudice in our lives. Through the shed Blood of Jesus Christ and the Holy Spirit, we have the power and ability to overcome all the works of the flesh, and that includes prejudice. We must learn to trust our Heavenly Father and become more than a conqueror through Jesus Christ.

For you are all sons of God through faith in Christ Jesus. **Galatians 3:26**

In Christ we are all the same. In Christ there is no difference in race, social status, economic status, male or female. So why do we have segregated churches? The family of God has done a terrible job of combating prejudice. The white folks worship over here and the black folks worship over there and the brown here and the red there. We have separated ourselves by color. I believe that sometimes we are afraid of different cultures. Sometimes the different customs of other cultures can be offensive to us, but as believers, you have to remember to respond correctly. White churches are known to be dead. Black churches are known to be too emotional. The Bible says as children of God, we need to be able to worship together. Churches should be filled with black, white, brown, yellow, and red people all coming together as part of the body of Christ. However, before this can occur, Christians need to overcome their prejudice.

When I was a kid, black people had to ride in the back of the bus. I can hardly imagine that in my mind. How can a Christian who knows that in Christ we are the same, be a part of such a thing? I believe that the average white person will never understand the hurts and degradation that black people have suffered over the years. All we can try to do is be a part of the solution and not the problem.

In the World Book it says that racism is one race that believes it is superior to another race. The example it uses is apartheid in South Africa. God is against any human oppression including apartheid, which is nothing more than another form of prejudice. As followers in Jesus Christ, we know that racism is contrary to the Word of God. As Christians we must not submit to the teachings of man, but to the Word of God.

The world has a way of affecting our attitudes. It molds us and puts prejudice inside us. The devil has a plan to bring prejudice into all our lives. Injustices, discriminations, and persecutions may come against you. However, when you are injured by an unjust act, you must determine in your heart not to let that hurt get down inside your spirit. If you do, you are headed toward destruction. In most cases, people who are prejudiced don't want to admit or recognize prejudice in their own life. Unfortunately you can still find prejudice in the church today, but we as Christians must take a stand against the sin of prejudice. None of us should be content until all barriers are broken between color lines. We will probably never change the world, but we can no longer allow the world to affect or change us. We must be determined to love one another.

"And He has made from one blood every nation of men to dwell on all the face of the earth, and has determined their preappointed times and the boundaries of their habitation." Acts 17:26

Acts 17:26 says that we are all of one blood. The blood of a black person and the blood of a white person is exactly the same. If you are really in Christ, you can't even see the outer layer of skin. Peter said that if we are born-again, we are a holy nation, a royal priesthood, a chosen generation, because we are the people of God.

White preachers have taught that the black race is cursed because of the sins of their forefathers. They are promoting racism in the church with the belief that somehow they are superior. Black preachers tell their congregation, "Don't go over to that white man's church."

We all need to be loved, encouraged, and accepted. Racism and prejudice produces hate, strife and division. That's why God hates racism because it is so against the gospel of Jesus Christ. If the gospel that you are being taught does not bring people together in love and unity, there is something wrong with the religion you are involved with.

Man judges others based on the exterior. Prejudice judges people by the color of their skin. God judges the thoughts and intentions of the heart. In Christ we are equal and there is no difference. Our God is for human rights and equality.

God is no respecter of persons. In Christ there is no partiality toward one particular race. Man will judge people based on the prejudice in his life, but God sees all people the same. God is not white. He is not black. God is Spirit, and Spirit has no color. God is neutral. The Church of God should be neutral also. Let it begin with you.

Chapter Two

Overcoming Hatred

"For many will come in My name, saying, 'I am the Christ,' and will mislead many. And you will be hearing of wars and rumors of wars; see that you are not frightened, for those things must take place, but that is not yet the end. For nation will rise against nation, and kingdom against kingdom, and in various places there will be famines and earthquakes. But all these things are merely the beginning of birth pangs. Then they will deliver you to tribulation, and will kill you, and you will be hated by all nations on account of My name. And at that time, many will fall away and will deliver up one another and hate one another. And many false prophets will rise, and will mislead many. And because lawlessness is increased, most people's love will grow cold." **Matthew 24:5-12**

Our Lord told us that this would be an example of things to come before He returns to this earth. All of these things are taking place right now, but let's focus on the fact that in the last days hatred will grow and people will hate one another. The Bible says that because of sin, love will stop and hatred will grow among people.

In our inner cities, the housing developments have become war zones. Even in our school systems, we see the gospel of hate and prejudice growing with the influx of the skin-heads, the gang members, the Black Muslims, and the KKK rallies. People are filled with hate as never before. In a day when we should be loving one another, we are hating one another.

Recently, Washington DC's Chief of Police resigned from the force. He said all the killing and all the hatred had finally gotten to him. He said, "I'm afraid if I stay in this job, I'll crack up." He told of police officers being killed in the line of duty during simple routine traffic checks. When he began on the force and confronted a burglar, the burglar would put the gun down. Now he states, that when his officers confront a burglar, they often find themselves face to face with a machine gun, and a man intent on killing them. Hatred in all our communities has become a deadly issue.

Hatred among people is growing at an alarming rate. Distrust between races has never been greater than today. Violence sparked by prejudice is growing out of control. Prejudice is what led to violence in the Rodney King controversy. Prejudice was evident on both sides of this situation. The police officers exhibited their prejudice through the racial remarks and severe and cruel beating of Rodney King. The Black

Community also allowed their prejudice and hate to grow out of control. Riots and violence resulted from pre-judging a race and the actions of a few.

I wish I could say the days of racism were over, but they are not. Incidents like the Rodney King issue show that prejudice is still prevalent in our society. Everywhere you turn you see racism coming to the forefront. Hispanics and the political bloc of Miami's Cuban immigrants feel persecuted. The Vietnamese boat people, the Haitian boat people, the Asian shop owners, all feel the effects of racism. Some Anglos feel threatened at the sight of a black man in their neighborhood. It's all a sign of the times. It's a sign of the end.

Develop A Servant's Heart

For you were called to freedom, brethren; only do not turn your freedom into an opportunity for the flesh, but through love serve one another. **Galatians 5:13**

The attitude of all Christians of all races ought to be "I'm here to serve my fellow man. I'm here to serve you in love." Love should come through the body of Christ, not through the world. If you could only understand *"Love your neighbor as yourself,"* you wouldn't have a problem with sin. If you loved your neighbor as yourself, you wouldn't do anything to hurt your neighbor, regardless of their color. You wouldn't get involved with sin because you know sin hurts and destroys and damages.

As Christians we must learn to overcome our pasts. When we accepted Jesus Christ as our Savior, our past was washed under the Blood. However, the more sin we have in our lives, the more problems we have. Sin creates problems. We're in a maturing process and part of that process is to learn how to forgive, to learn to get bitterness out of us, and refuse to allow hatred to operate through us.

The Christian walk isn't just overcoming our past, but overcoming the works of the flesh that want to operate through us everyday. Our flesh has an ungodly nature and even though we desire to operate in the Spirit, the pull of this world is strong. When we choose hatred over love, we choose to walk in our flesh. When we deliberately set out to hurt someone or in some way try to get even with them, we have allowed hatred to take us captive. Our prisons are full of people who have permitted hatred to take them over.

Dr. Sumrall wrote a book entitled <u>Exorcism.</u> In that book he told about a woman who came to his church demon-possessed. They had an altar call and a demon inside her with a man's voice began to speak and the voice said, "This world is full of hatred and the power of that hatred is my strength." If you allow hatred to operate in you, you have given the enemy the very fuel that he needs to destroy you and your family.

Hatred is the nature of Satan himself and is an ugly thing to witness. God says if you don't turn from hatred, you will not inherit the Kingdom of God. And if you give into hatred, you will say and do some very ridiculous things. One of the things you will do is talk about others in a way that can damage them or hurt their reputation. If you are not careful, revenge and vengeance will take you over. You will lay in bed at night tormented with the thoughts of revenge and hatred toward that individual.

God's Word says to give no place to the devil. If you refuse to walk in love, hatred will take you over, and it is the very device the enemy will use to destroy you. If you make up your mind to forgive and walk in love the enemy's strategy to bring destruction into your life will be stopped.

You Have a Choice

What do you do if someone hurts you or is prejudiced against you? Life is a series of choices.

God's Word says that everyday we choose the blessing or the curse, life or death, prosperity or adversity. God has set these things before us. We have a choice of what we do. We can be angry in our mind, but in our spirit, we can choose to react the way God would have us react.

> *Bless those who persecute you; bless and curse not....Never pay back evil for evil to anyone. Respect what is right in the sight of all men.* **Romans 12:14, 17**

Some Christians believe they can pick and choose what scriptures apply to their lives. Especially when they find themselves in circumstances where they feel uncomfortable or in situations that don't line up with God's Word. The Bible says never pay back evil for evil...be at peace with *all* men. There may be times when you have a personality conflict with someone and they just don't like you. Their actions plainly display that they don't want to be at peace with you. However, your attitude needs to reflect God's love and peace. As a born-again Christian contention must not come from you.

The nature of the flesh is Satan's nature. You can't go by how you feel. Whenever love prevails, the stronghold of hell is torn down and the enemy is disarmed. Love will always turn the arrows of hate and prejudice, eventually. When you don't forgive people for the things they do, a seed of bitterness begins to grow inside of you. That bitterness will eventually become anger. And if the anger stays, it will grow into hatred. Forgiveness and walking in love is the only answer for a Christian. That's why you must deal with anger the very moment it occurs. The Bible says, "Don't let the sun go down on your anger." Forgive immediately. That way you don't allow it to fester and get down on the inside of you.

If you instantly forgive those who hurt you, hatred and prejudice will never operate in your life. That's the only smart way to live. If you allow unforgiveness and hatred to go unchecked, it will eventually bring pain and destruction into your life. In spite of the pain and misery you bring into this earthly life because you refuse to forgive, God's Word tells us that the bottom line to unforgiveness is...you won't inherit the Kingdom of God.

A soldier who served in Vietnam came home with tremendous problems. He was wounded in the war and had an extreme hatred for all oriental people. This hatred brought nothing but more pain and suffering into his life. Until he made a choice to forgive those who had hurt him, he was never able to receive God's peace and joy.

No matter who you are, you will never be an overcoming Christian unless you overcome the nature of your flesh. Every one of us has a dark side to our nature, but the devil can never defeat a Christian who has his flesh submitted to the Word of God.

Prejudice Breeds Hate And Distrust

This world is full of people who don't forgive and are hurting, angry, bitter, and hateful. But our God expects us to be different than the world and He expects us to be an instrument of love and healing for a hurting humanity.

I know a family whose skin color is white. Their home was broken into by some young black men. Now they have a tremendous hatred for all black people. I know a black family whose daughter was raped by a white man. Now they hate all white people. These people are experiencing an irrational suspicion that has grown into the hatred of an entire race of people. They have become prejudiced.

Anytime a wrong is perpetrated against you, you have a choice...either get bitter and begin to hate, or you can forgive and overlook it and get better. The problem with hate is that it gives your spiritual enemy power to destroy you. It's always you that ends up the loser. You end up bitter and full of hate. People full of hate always live in the past. They relive every past hurt they've ever had over and over and over again. What a death sentence to continually relive, in your mind, all of the hurt and pain somebody caused you 10 years ago or whatever.

For some reason, we tend to judge a particular group of people because of the actions of a few. When you judge someone in this manner that judgment is based on fear. Women who have been sexually abused can be afraid of men, or one race of people can be afraid of another race of people. *U. S. News and World Report* July 1991 said prejudice, racism, and segregation is growing in our country. The problems in minority communities are growing at an unprecedented rate. The statistics are awful and the problems are many.

Racism and prejudice is the way of this world. People hate and prejudge one another, but our God expects more from us than that. This world is not going to change, but you and I must. It is the responsibility of the church to love and to bless others.

Hate will poison you and everyone around you. If you walk around your house with hatred in your heart, it poisons everyone in your house. As our children mature, they often take on the attitudes and actions of those around them. Prejudice is a learned behavior. Prejudice was introduced into your life in the same manner. Somewhere along the line, someone taught you to be prejudiced with their words or their actions. Prejudice was fed into your spirit and became entrenched inside of you.

Love Your Enemies

There was a white family that moved into a racially mixed neighborhood. The child went to school and came home and the mother asked, "Are there any colored children in your class?" The child answered, "What color?" If we truly want the Kingdom of God operating in our lives, we have to become like children. Children see no color.

You ask, how do you forgive someone? With love! Love is kind. Love bears all things, love endures all things. Love never fails. Love overlooks wrongs and love overlooks hurts that people inflict upon you.

Jesus said, *"Love your enemies."* He wasn't talking about kissing them, but an attitude of walking in love. He was talking about instantly forgiving and not letting a seed of bitterness get inside you.

When people love and forgive each other, the power of God is released. When love is released, the enemy's power is neutralized. Forgiveness releases the power of God, hatred unleashes the power of Satan.

Make up your mind never to be a part of anything that hurts the body of Christ. Put aside hate and prejudice. Love will cause the church to expand and become more powerful. Anytime there is a decrease in love, there is an increase in demonic activity. Whenever love and grace abound, the power of Satan is broken.

God says if you allow hatred to operate in your life, you won't inherit the Kingdom of God. What is the Kingdom of God? Righteousness, peace, and joy. It's walking in the Spirit. You don't have a chance to walk in the Spirit unless you submit to God on a daily basis because the deeds of the flesh will operate through you. He's the vine and you are the branches. You draw your life from Him.

"I am the true vine, and My Father is the vinedresser. Every branch in Me that does not bear fruit, He takes away; and every branch that bears fruit, He prunes it, that it may bear more fruit. You are already clean because of the Word which I have spoken to you. Abide in Me and I in you. As the branch cannot bear fruit of itself, unless it abides in the vine , so neither can you, unless you abide in Me. I am the vine, you are the branches; He who abides in Me, and I in him, he bears much fruit; for apart from Me you can do nothing. If anyone does not abide in Me, he

is thrown away as a branch, and dries up; and they gather them, and cast them into the fire, and they are burned. If you abide in Me, and My words abide in you, ask whatever you wish, and it shall be done for you. By this is My Father glorified, that you bear much fruit, and so prove to be My disciples. Just as the Father has loved Me, I have also loved you; abide in My love. If you keep My commandments, you will abide in My love; just as I have kept my Father's commandments, and abide in His love."

John 15:1-10

If you are not abiding in the Word of God, chances are you have very little good fruit in your life. You may be saved and you may be going to heaven, but you are not producing good fruit. We are just a branch of the Vine. We draw life from Him. If we are not abiding in Him, we don't have the strength to love like He loves. So if we abide in Him, He gives us the ability to love. You have to make the choice to reach out to people that you would have never reached out to before. Hug people that are different than you. You can no longer remain content to stay in your comfort zone. You must make up your mind to step out in faith and reach out in love.

We won't be divided by denominations in heaven.

Church doctrine is not what it's all about. Abiding in Jesus Christ is everything. It is a threefold relationship. You abiding in Christ, Him abiding in you, and you abiding in His love.

To live a victorious Christian life, you must make the choice to overcome evil with good, overcome bitterness with forgiveness, overcome hatred with love, and release all of your hurts into the hands of your loving Heavenly Father.

By this all men will know that you are My disciples, if you have love for one another.
John 13:35

God's love draws men and women to Him. He doesn't sort people by color. His grace flows toward all of His children. How can we as the body of Christ ever hope to display God's love to a lost and dying world when we can't even love one another because of the pigmentation of our skin?

"For God so loved the world, that He gave His only begotten Son, that whoever believes in Him should not perish, but have eternal life."
John 3:16

In other words, God loves the world, and that

means all people. If you think that God loves one race of people more than another, you are greatly mistaken.

We are supposed to be the family of God, and as a family, we are to love each other, treat each other with respect, and share in each other's sorrows and triumphs. Instead of being a family, the church is separated, segregated, and divided.

We need to change our goals. We must learn to build one another up and not tear one another down. When the love of God is in our hearts, we will embrace people of all races and colors.

Chapter Three

We are all the Same in Christ

For you are all sons and daughters through faith in Christ Jesus. For all of you who are baptized into Christ and clothed yourselves with Christ. There is neither Jew nor Greek neither slave nor free man. You are all one in Christ Jesus. If you belong to Christ, then you are Abraham's offspring and heirs according to promise. *Galatians 3:26-29*

We are all the same in Christ. There is neither Jew nor Greek, neither slave nor free man, neither black nor white, neither brown nor yellow nor red. The Bible says that if we belong to Christ, then we are Abraham's offspring...children of God...heirs according to His promise. In other words, God's Word is for you, no matter what race or color you are. The same promises that belonged to Abraham belong to you.

The Breakdown Of The American Family

There are lots of problems in the world...family problems, gang problems, drug problems. Fifty-seven percent of all the youth of America are without a father in their home. In ninety percent of all single parent homes the mother is the head of the household and the children are left with virtually no male influence in their lives. There is a breakdown in the American family and it is not exclusive to one race or color. Families are being pulled apart and their only hope is life through Christ Jesus.

No matter who you are, God's Word is for you. God is not mad at you. He sent Jesus to die for you and His blessings are for all of you who call on the name of the Lord. If you are a minority, the odds may be greatly against you today, but if you love Jesus Christ, the Bible says that you are more than a conqueror through Him who loves you. If God be for you, who can be against you. God is so big that He will take what the enemy meant to destroy you with and turn it for your good.

Perhaps you have experienced the hate of prejudice in your life, and you ask, how can God turn that for my good? As you sell out to Him and determine to forgive those who have hurt you, He will bring love, peace and joy into your life. There is hope through the family of God and through the shed Blood of Jesus Christ. Life will never be a bed of roses, and people will still hurt you, however, you can rise above the problems of life because you have been adopted into the family of God.

Spirit of Adoption

For all who are being led by the Spirit of God, these are sons of God. For you have not received a spirit of slavery leading to fear again, but you have received a Spirit of adoption as sons by which we cry out, "Abba! Father!" **Romans 8:14-15**

God leads His people by His Spirit. Until you came to know Jesus Christ, you were led by a spirit of slavery and bondage. The spirit of bondage is the nature of our enemy, Satan. The spirit of adoption is the nature of God. When you received Jesus into your life as Lord and Savior, the nature of God was imparted to you, no matter your color. Once you asked Jesus to be Lord of your life, you became a part of the body of Christ. John 1:12 states, *But as many as received Him, to them He gave the right to become children of God, even to those who believe in His name.* With Christ in your life, you are a part of the family of God!

Now I say, as long as the heir is a child, he does not differ at all from a slave although he is owner of everything, but he is under guardians and managers until the date set by the Father, so also we, while we were children, were held in bondage under the elemental things of the world.

But when the fullness of the time came, God sent forth His son, born of a woman, born under the law, in order that He might redeem those who were under the law, that we might receive the adoption as sons. And because you are sons, God has sent forth the Spirit of His son into our hearts, crying, "Abba! Father!" Therefore, you are no longer a slave, but a son; and if a son, then an heir through God. **Galatians 4:1-7**

Through Jesus you can now call God the Father, "Daddy." You used to be a slave to sin. You can now overcome the spirit of slavery and bondage in your life with the spirit of adoption. You are an heir through God with rights and privileges.

You have a Father who loves you and you are joint heirs with your Big Brother, Jesus. You have the same rights and privileges as the other brothers and sisters in the same family...black, white, brown, yellow, or red. Call on your Big Brother when you need help. He can whip anybody! Especially the devil! My Big Brother said He'd never leave me nor forsake me.

Chosen Race

But you are a chosen race, a royal priesthood, a holy nation, a people for God's own possession that you may proclaim the excellencies of Him who has called you out of darkness into His marvelous light. **1 Peter 2:9**

In the 1960's, black people had an identity crisis within themselves not knowing exactly their roots and heritage. It was important to them to know about their heritage. We all have a sense of pride as we identify with a group or nationality of people.

Even if you don't know who your ancestors were, your roots were in Jesus Christ when you became born-again. People have always been proud of their heritage, but when you came into the family of God, your identity changed. The spirit of adoption was present in your life....and your identity became the Family of God. You are a Christian first and foremost, a chosen race, a part of a royal priesthood.

God the Father is the landowner and Jesus is our Big Brother and Chief Shepherd and we are the sheep of His pasture. We are all in the body of Christ. We may have different colors of wool, but we are all a part of the same flock and the sheep of the same pasture. We belong to Him.

Since we are a part of one family, we ought to act like we are one family. Don't place us in a white church or a black church. We are one Church in the body of Jesus Christ. We must learn to love the other sheep in the pasture because we are going to spend eternity with them.

Chapter Four

Enlarging Your Circle of Love

Set your mind on the things above, not on the things that are on earth. For you have died and your life is hidden with Christ in God. When Christ, who is our life, is revealed, then you also will be revealed with Him in glory. Therefore consider the members of your earthly body as dead to immortality, impurity, passion, evil desire, and greed, which amounts to idolatry. For it is on account of these things that the wrath of God will come, and in them you also once walked, when you were living in them. But now you also, put them all aside: anger, wrath, malice, slander, and abusive speech from your mouth. Do not lie to one another, since you laid aside the old self with it's evil practices, and have put on the new self who is being renewed to a true knowledge according to the image of the one who created him - a renewal in which there is no distinction between Greek and Jew, circumcised and uncircumcised, barbarian, Scythian, slave and freeman, but Christ is all, and in all. And so, as those who have been chosen of God, holy and beloved, put on a heart

of compassion, kindness, humility, gentleness, and patience; bearing with one another, and forgiving each other, whoever has a complaint against anyone; just as the Lord forgave you, so also should you. And beyond all these things put on love, which is the perfect bond of unity.
Colossians 3:2-14

Prejudice never solves problems. The only solution is following Jesus and walking in forgiveness and love. We need each other to receive love and acceptance. That's why the church needs to be a safe place...a place for all people to gather to worship the Lord.

Love is the shield that turns back the arrows of hatred and prejudice. That is the secret. You must enlarge your circle of love to include everyone, no matter their color. You will have a hard time if you try to do it yourself. You need the God kind of love flowing within you.

Everyone has a circle of love. We love our friends and our family. However, there are very few who like to be pushed out of their comfort zone. It's hard to love those you disagree with or those who disagree with you. But the God kind of love embraces all people. The God kind of love enlarges your circle of love.

The God Kind Of Love

If someone says, "I love God," and hates his brother, he is a liar; for the one who does not love his brother whom he has seen, cannot love God whom he has not seen. **1 John 4:20**

Human love is a very weak and frail thing. Godly love loves people in spite of situations. Godly love will bring those into their circle that nobody else will love. Godly love will embrace those who look different and act different than us. Godly love will enlarge a circle to include all people. We cannot exclude anyone from the love of God. You can say you love God, but if you don't love the man or woman of a different race then you are a liar. When you put someone outside your circle of love, you are operating in your flesh. You are allowing the enemy to bring division into the body of Christ.

Beloved, let us love one another, for love is from God; and every one who loves is born of God and knows God. **1 John 4:7**

God desires for you to be the light for this world and let your light shine wherever you work and wherever you play. How do you let your light shine? The best way I know is to love people. Love those who don't deserve to be loved. Love those who don't look like you think they should look or act like you think they should act. It's time for every one of us to enlarge our circle of love and to embrace all people with the love of God.

If you know God, you will love. **1 John 4:8**

The Bible doesn't say, "If you know God, you will love those you like." It says, "If you know God, you will love"...period. You cannot exclude anyone from the circle of love in your life. Religion will exclude lots of people. Religion says that if you don't go to the same church that I go to, get out of here, I don't want to associate with you. Christianity is joy, peace, love, and kindness. People cannot resist genuine love. I don't care what color their skin is, they cannot resist love. Whenever you find God and His love, you'll find growth and new life. Everything our Lord touches multiplies and lives.

Jesus never shut off His circle of love. Even when they hung Him on the cross, He forgave them. He included the soldiers in His circle of love as He died. Jesus included Judas in His circle of love. Does your circle include those who would betray you, or just those you like? Loving everybody is going to take you out of your comfort zone.

God commands us to love. John 13:34 says, *"A new*

commandment I give to you, that you love one another, even as I have loved you, that you also love one another." Love is a choice. You can do as God says, or you can ignore His Word and His Will for your life. It's your decision. Spend time with God and His love will overtake you. Perhaps you feel you don't know how to love. Love is a decision and as you reach out to others, His love will flow through you.

Chapter Five

Church of All Nations

There is great persecution today toward any minority group. The Polish people are greatly oppressed in this country. In some parts of our country, the Italians and Mexicans are oppressed. There is a tremendous resurgence of hatred toward the Japanese people.

Hitler's notion was that Jews were inferior, and that same prejudice exists today. American Nazis are beating up Jewish kids in New York just because they are Jews. In Dallas, there is a special hatred against Jewish Christians.

Prejudice occurs in all parts of the world. The world is against Jesus-people, no matter what their color. The church needs to be a safe place. The church must learn to resist prejudice, hatred and bitterness. Where sin abounds, grace abounds much more. The world may be getting further from God, but as Christians the closer we draw to God, the more we become like Jesus. The more we are like Jesus, the more we will love each other and encourage one another and build each other up.

I'm very much aware of the prejudice and injustices against minorities. We're all human. We all fail. We all need Jesus to change us. Forgiveness is necessary if you are going to go on with God. You must forgive people of other races and colors that have hurt you. You will never become what God wants you to be unless you forgive others.

The Lord spoke to me and said, "How can a church call themselves a Jesus Church if they are an all-white church or an all-black church? One of the greatest reasons black people and white people worship separately is due to a lack of trust between races. How can we call ourselves disciples of Jesus Christ when we are segregated in our churches?" "How can we ever hope to affect a city, when the body of Christ is so divided?"

The Bible is very clear, once you get past the first layer of skin, we are all the same. The blood of the human race is all the same whether it comes from a black man or a white man. Our cultures may be different, but we should rejoice in our differences. God's Word says, that the body is made up of different members.

For the body is not one member, but many....That there should be no division in the body, but that the members should have the same care for one another. **1 Corinthians 12:14, 25**

It is especially important that preachers put down their differences with other churches and other preachers. We must learn to love one another from the pulpit as well as the pew.

If the church will put down its differences, the end result will be a tremendous harvest of souls. Unless we come together in love, things will not get better and prejudice will grow. We must eliminate all forms of racism and prejudice from our lives. The body of Christ must begin to worship together, regardless of their race or nationality. Skin color means nothing to God, and as a child of God, you cannot allow racial hatred of any kind in your heart.

Love and Equality

God raised up Martin Luther King to stand in the gap. He laid his life on the line to bring equality to all people. He brought great advances to our country, by speaking forth Godly principles to the nation. From Stone Mountain, Georgia, he stood up to the nation and declared, "I have a dream." Dr. King had a dream that human beings were to be treated equally and have equal rights. The dream was that all men could worship God together, all men could work together, that all men and women would be equal. As the church we should share that same dream. We should dream to see God's power move and touch all people no matter what their color, their status, their size, or their shape.

Dr. King knew how to reach that dream. He told the people, "I will call on the name of the Lord and the Lord will deliver us." He was a man after God's own heart. He had a vision of equal rights for all people. God's Word was a mighty sword for Dr. King. He knew God's Word was true and as he stood in the gap, God heard his prayers.

Dr. King gave his life and became a living sacrifice so that great advancements would be accomplished in the area of equality. Dr. King brought the message of God's love to hurting people. He delivered the message of the cross of Jesus Christ to hurting humanity. The message that Jesus came to make all men and women free. The message that Jesus is the only answer to man's problems. Dr. King preached the same message that Jesus Christ brought to us.

> *Then Peter opened his mouth and said: In truth I perceive that God shows no partiality, but in every nation whoever fears Him and works righteousness is accepted by Him." Acts 10:34,35*

It is interesting to note that God gave three great men the same vision. In Acts 10:34, 35 God showed Peter a church for all nations. Pastor Seymour's message during the Azuza Street Revival was that racial prejudice was not for the body of Christ and Dr. King told a bigoted world of God's great love and his vision for unity among the races.

Unfortunately the world has not been able to receive this message. The message of love and reconciliation cannot be received until we have the ability to conquer all works of the flesh through Jesus. We can overcome only through the Blood of Jesus Christ.

Jesus came to bring equal rights to all people. We have a right to be healed, saved and restored, regardless of the color of our skin. We all know we live in a racist society. The church of Jesus Christ must stop thinking like a white church, black church, or a brown church. We are the people of God, called by His name, called out of darkness and delivered from shame by the precious Blood of Jesus Christ. It is the shed Blood of Jesus that washes away barriers of prejudice and color.

His Blood will change you if you will let it. His Blood will wash you clean if you will let it. This world needs a Blood transfusion...the Blood of Jesus Christ.

As born-again believers in Christ, we not only have the opportunity to conquer prejudice in our own lives, our families, our churches, but we have an absolute command from God to do so. God raised up a black man at the beginning of this century and He's doing the same thing at the close of this century. The decade of the 1990's will see people of color rise to the forefront. I believe with all my heart that we have entered the last decade and will see the return of our Lord and Savior, Jesus Christ.

The end times church must be a church for all people. We know that in Christ we are all the same. We are in the last days. United we stand and divided we fall. When the body of Christ comes together we will be stronger. Churches that are reaching out to all races, all colors, all nations, are the churches that the anointing of God is going to rest upon. There is a wave of evangelism coming in this last decade that is going to astound the world. We should not be a black church, white church, but a church for all people, all races, all denominations.

It is time for the church to become the church and quit playing church. Religion will adjust itself to society, but God's Word never changes. His standards are the same today as they were 2,000 years ago in Acts 10.

Ninety years ago God began to pull down walls of racial hatred and segregation. He wants to bring prejudice to an end in your life. Are you willing to submit to God's Word? The Lord can only use someone whose heart is open to all races.

Our spiritual enemy hates us all and will do anything he can to keep us from loving each other and to keep us from accepting one another. He uses labels to separate people and keep them divided. I am not the color white. Indians are not the color red. Black people are not the color black. The devil knows that a house united can stand against anything, especially him. United we are strong. When the churches unite together in love and unity, you will see a mighty harvest of souls. God is tearing down the walls of prejudice inside His church today. Jesus said, that they will know us by our love. He didn't say that they would know us by the size of our church buildings. That means you are going to have to forgive people of a particular race if you are going to become what God wants you to become.

Prejudice isn't so much a skin thing as it is a sin thing. Hatred has existed from the very beginning. The devil has always been behind strife, envy, jealousy, and division. Prejudice has always been with us, not just in America. Men have oppressed other men for thousands of years, always wanting to control others.

The devil wants to control and be in control. The Jews were slaves to the Egyptians. In Jesus' day the Samaritans were greatly despised and hated because they were of mixed blood.

> *For even as the body is one and yet has many members, and all the members of the body, though they are many, are one body, so also is Christ.* **1 Corinthians 12:12**

Do you think there is prejudice in heaven? Do you think there will be a black section and a white section? Jesus said, *"Thy will be done on earth as it is in heaven."* If there is no prejudice in heaven, then it is His will that there be no prejudice on this earth...especially in His church.

The body of Christ can no longer be divided. We must stand our ground against racism, prejudice and segregation.

> *"If, however, you are fulfilling the royal law, according to the Scripture, You shall love your neighbor as yourself," you are doing well. But if you show partiality, you are committing sin and are convicted by the law as transgressors."* **James 2:8,9**

Prejudice of any kind leaves no room for love or

tolerance. You must determine in your heart that you are either going to follow God or our spiritual enemy. Choose between the blessing or the curse.

If you have a problem with prejudice, you need to repent and spend time with God so He can change you.

For when My people who are called by My name will humble themselves and pray and seek My face and turn from their wicked ways, then I will hear from heaven, will forgive their sin, and will heal their land. II Chronicles 7:14

We serve a God of love and as His children we can no longer keep people outside of our circle of love. If you truly desire God's Will for your life, I ask you to take a moment and search your heart for any prejudice or unforgiveness that might be present. Then if you truly want to repent and walk in the blessings of our Lord please pray this short prayer on the following page:

Prayer

I confess Jesus Christ as Lord. I believe that he died for my sins, and God raised Him from the dead. Father, I especially ask You to forgive me for the sin of prejudice in my life. I repent and turn from that sin as an act of my will. I ask You to place a new love in my heart for all people. Father, I know prejudice is a work of the enemy in my life, and I know that You desire for me to reach out in love to all people, no matter their ethnic background or skin color. Lord, You know I have hurts in my life that have caused me to walk in unforgiveness, I give those hurts to You and I ask You to heal my life. Father, I give You my life as a living sacrifice. I desire to be all You want me to be. I choose today to walk in love toward all people. In Jesus Name I pray. AMEN

Additional Ministry Materials Available

If you are interested in purchasing additional teaching material by Pastor Dennis Leonard, we have included a catalog of cassette tapes and books for your convenience. (Order form available on page 64)

Pastor Leonard may also be seen on the LeSea Network in many areas of the country and on Channel 20 on cable stations in the Denver Area. Check your local television listings for time and location.

Four Pack Tape Series
Audio Cassettes
$15.00 Each Set

Title   **Order Number**

Overcoming Depression   **SA 104**

Thousands of people suffer from depression today. Depression is not only an issue in the secular world, it is also in the church. If depression is stealing your joy, as well as your relationship with God, this dynamic tape series will help guide you on a path to joy and happiness through Christ Jesus.

Overcoming Fear   **SA 105**

We live in a world that is dominated by fear...fear of death, fear of loneliness, fear of getting old, fear of not having enough money. If you are worried or fearful, then you are not being ruled by God. This tape series will help you find the truth in God's Word to overcoming fear in your life.

Overcoming Rejection   **SA 106**

One of the most powerful emotions one can feel, is the pain of rejection, which comes from not being accepted and being denied love. If the enemy can succeed in bruising innocent victims, he can lead people to lives of emotional instability, and broken relationships that can continue for a lifetime. This series of tapes will help you live a victorious life and overcome your feelings of rejection.

What God Says About Sex   **SA 107**

This powerful series examines God's Word on the World's Sexual Revolution. We live in a sexually oriented society that is obsessed with sex and encourages everyone to be sexually active. If you are confused on what God's Word says about this subject, this series will help you understand God's will for your life.

Touching God Through Prayer   **SA 111**

If you want to see the power of God in your life you must be committed to prayer. Many people misunderstand prayer, they simply think it is a weapon to use against the devil, but it is more than that, it is a daily relationship between you and God. This series on prayer will help you develop a stronger and closer relationship with the Lord.

Four Pack Tape Series - Continued
Audio Cassettes
$15.00 Each Set

Title	Order Number

Pride - God Is Opposed To The Proud SA 112

Pride was the original sin of Lucifer. The nature of the flesh is to be proud. God says, "He gives grace to the humble." Pride is very deceiving, most people can see pride working in someone else's life but not in their own. We all have areas of pride in our life, this revealing tape series will help us look at that pride and gain new understanding; thereby bringing healing and restoration into all or our lives.

Overcoming Worry SA 113

The Christian walk is one of learning to trust God in spite of the circumstances of life. Worry is defined as a form of fear. This life changing tape series will show you how to live above the circumstances of life, and put God in charge.

The Blood Of Jesus SA 115

God has given us five weapons in which to combat the enemy. The Blood of Jesus is one of these powerful weapons. This authoritative tape series will help you understand the covenant the Lord has given us, and the power that is in the precious Blood of Jesus Christ.

Bring On The Joy SA 116

God's Word says, "To enter His gates with thanksgiving in your mouth." This tape series will teach you the power of Praise and Worship. Praise will release faith into your life and through faith God will meet your needs. Praise and Worship is one of the most important aspects of our Christian walk, yet most Christians spend very little time in actual Praise and Worship. If you need a miracle from God this tape series is a must.

Forgiveness SA 117

We live in a world that is full of hate and anger. People live bruised and destroyed lives because of unforgiveness. This tape packet will show you how to overcome the hurts of this life and release them to our Heavenly Father. If you know someone who is caught in the grips of despair, this tape series will help bring healing and restoration to their life.

Four Pack Tape Series - Continued
Audio Cassettes
$15.00 Each Set

Title **Order Number**

Divorce Recovery SA 123

We live in a society where divorce is running rampant. The pain and heartbreak of divorce is like no other. No one seems exempt from this modern day blight which is effecting our land. This tape series deals directly with the needs of divorce victims in a head-on and loving manner.

Be Careful What You Say SA 124

The words of your mouth either brings death or life to a situation. Jesus says in Matthew 15:11, "It is not what enters a man's mouth that defiles him, but what comes out of his mouth." When you talk about your situation in a negative manner you will eventually seal your own destiny. This exciting and revealing tape series will teach you to speak faith out of your mouth. God responds to our faith. This principle alone will teach you how to live a victorious Christian life.

Mini Tape Series
Audio Cassettes

Finances SA 122

This tape series will teach you how to manage your money God's way and use your faith for your finances. God has great blessings for us, however our spiritual enemy has a plan to stop those blessings. If you are having difficulty in your finances this 3 part tape series is based on sound Biblical principles and will help bring healing into your finances.
Cost......$15.00

Overcoming Low Self-Esteem SA 127

God wants to impart His life and abilities to you, so you can live a healthy, happy, and prosperous life. Jesus came to let you know that you are important and valuable to Him. If life has you believing that you are not worth much, and you have lost your hope, this 2 part series will bring forth God's Word of healing and restoration for your life.
Cost......$10.00

Six Pack Tape Series
Audio Cassettes
$25.00 Each Set

Title	Order Number

The Power Of Love   SA 101

This powerful and anointed tape series will teach you how to enlarge your circle of love. People cannot resist love, because everyone desperately needs to be loved. When you are in Christ, you cannot exclude anyone from your circle of love. This dynamic tape series will teach you how to overlook all offenses, and become a world changer and people lifter.

Marriage and The Family   SA 102

Our spiritual enemy has a plan to destroy every Christian family and marriage. Jesus said, "A house divided cannot stand." This tape series will bring laughter as Pastor Dennis discusses the many differences between men and women, and will also bring healing to broken marriages and hurting families.

Jesus   SA 121

There is one name under heaven that has all authority and power and that name is Jesus. This exciting tape series will give you a personal glimpse of our Messiah. Titles such as Jesus Has The Name, Building Upon The Rock, The Good News of Jesus, The Resurrection And The Life, Christ Living In Me, and There's A Lion On The Inside Of Me, will show you that Jesus loves you and He's come to give you life. New Christians and mature Christians alike will benefit from these teachings.

Overcoming The Flesh   SA 125

There are areas in everyone's life that need a little fixing up. Maybe you were brought up in a home that taught you to be prejudiced, or perhaps you know someone who has trouble telling the truth and you have been looking for a way to help them. Are you feeling discouraged, or do you find yourself being critical and judgemental? If you need help in any of these areas or perhaps you know someone that is searching for a way to overcome some of these things in their life, this tape series will be a blessing.

Six Pack Tape Series - Continued
Audio Cassettes
$25.00 Each Set

Title   **Order Number**

Getting Through Tough Times   **SA 126**
Everyone of us are faced with different struggles in our life. Very often we pray and become impatient wondering why God doesn't seem to be moving on our behalf. The tape series Getting Through Tough Times will help teach you how to give your burdens to God, so that He can turn your tribulation into triumph.

Spiritual Warfare   **SA 108**
The enemy has a plan to destroy your life, we must be ready before the attacks come. Pastor Dennis' tapes will help you become armed and dangerous when dealing with the enemy's attacks.

The Holy Spirit   **SA 109**
If you have questions on the Baptism of the Holy Spirit, speaking in tongues, or the gifts of the Spirit this informative tape series is for you. Pastor Dennis' teachings on the Holy Spirit will help you gain new understanding of the anointing and the power of the Holy Spirit and why you need this power in your life.

The Last Days   **SA 110**
Make no mistake Jesus is coming back soon! This exciting tape series will examine World Events, the New Age Movement, the 10 Nation Confederacy, the New World Order, and the signs of our Lord's return. If you enjoy prophecy or have questions about the Rapture or the Second Coming of our Lord this timely series is for you.

Grace   **SA 118**
This series is based on God's grace and love for His children. It will bring healing and restoration into the lives of many who feel they have committed the unpardonable sin. It will also minister to those who have served God at one time and feel they have failed, and God can't possibly forgive them again. Pastor Dennis shows through the Word, God's ever present love and continued forgiveness for His children.

Six Pack Tape Series - Continued
Audio Cassettes
$25.00 Each Set

Title   **Order Number**

Growing Up In Christ   **SA 119**
When we were first saved we could get a away with a lot more than we can now. We all need to remember growing up in Christ is a life long process. Many people want to know why life isn't working for them. God is calling His children to grow up in Christ. This insightful series will help you mature so that you can be everything God has called you to be, and receive all that God has for you.

Healing   **SA 120**
If you need healing in your body or in your life, this dynamic tape series will teach you God's principles for receiving your healing. Healing is for today and it is for you. God's Word says, "That He sent His Word and healed you." It is God's Will that you be healed. Sickness and disease are sent by our spiritual enemy. If you are believing God for your healing, this tape series can help set you free from bondage, torment and sickness.

Books
$5.00 Each

Title   **Order Number**

If God Can Forgive You...You Can Forgive Yourself   **B 101**
Focuses on God's forgiveness and unconditional love for His children. Once an individual realizes the extent of God's love, he or she understands, *If God can Forgive Me, I Can Forgive Myself.*

Overcoming Depression   **B 102**
If the enemy is stealing your joy, as well as your relationship with the Lord, this book will help you learn to become an "overcomer," and triumph over the enemy's plan to destroy your life through loneliness and depression.

Overcoming Fear   **B 103**
The message in this book will show you how God would have you deal with worry and fear in your life. It is God's desire for you to overcome the worries and fears of this life, and live victorious over the enemy.

Single Audio Cassettes
$5.00 Each

Title	Order Number
The Blood of Jesus	
Power In the Blood	A 333
This Blood's For You	A 494
The Blood Is A Mighty Weapon	A 528
The Precious Blood Of Jesus Christ	A 644
Finances	
Using Faith For Your Finances	A 458
Managing Your Money God's Way	A 630
The War Over Your Finances	A 632
Faith	
Legalism vs. Grace	A 646
Going Into Your Promised Land	A 651
Building Faith Muscles	A 652
Don't Live A Roller Coaster Life	A 653
Planting Good Seed	A 660
Stirring Up Your Faith	A 670
If God Be For Me	A 675
I'm Never Look Back	A 676
Carrying The Burdens Of Life	A 682
Faith Believes What You Can't See	A 703
Maturing In Our Faith	A 705
Family	
A House Divided	A 498
Lust, Sex And Love	A 515
Building A Strong Marriage	A 529
One Flesh Marriage	A 551
The Buffalo And The Butterfly	A 601
Marriage Is A Team Effort	A 645
Life After Divorce	A 658
Don't Be Unequally Yoked	A 679
Generational Sins And Curses	A 694
Sexual Fulfillment	A 697
Forgiveness	
Starting Over	A 512
Forgiveness Or Torment	A 530
Tearing Down Walls Of Unforgiveness	A 575
Forgiveness And Overcoming Your Past	A 606
Forgiveness What's Done Is Done	A 639
Overcoming Life	
Overcoming Anger	A 634
Uprooting Judgemental Attitudes	A 637
The Breaking Of Our Pride	A 638
Overcoming Closet Christianity	A 649
It's Not Good To Be Alone	A 657
Lying Lips	A 662
Defeating The Accuser	A 672
The Words Of Your Mouth	A 677
Prejudice In The Church	A 695
Overcoming Hatred	A 696
Grace To The Humble	A 698
Don't Lose Your Hope	A 700
A Fresh Start	A 702

Single Audio Cassettes - Continued
$5.00 Each

Title	Order Number

Growing Up In Christ

Giving Up Control	A	597
The Blessing Or The Curse	A	602
Blaming God	A	619
The Person God Uses	A	626
Struggles Make Us Stronger	A	633
Defeating The Accuser	A	672
Bearing Good Fruit	A	669
Turning Tribulation Into Triumph	A	673
Faithfulness, God's Key To Promotion	A	683
Following God's Authority	A	685
Glass Houses	A	686
The Lord Needs What You Have	A	687
Excuses - We All Have Them	A	688
Righteousness, Holiness and Sanctification	A	689
Facing The Gallows Of Life	A	690
Breaking Self-Sufficiency	A	699

Healing

The Miracle Jesus	A	474
Miracles Still Happen	A	538
Receiving Your Miracle	A	546
Laying On Of Hands	A	550
Healing For The Rejected	A	576
My Miracle Is In Progress	A	614
Following God's Authority	A	685
He's Still In The Healing Business	A	704

Holy Spirit

Increasing The Anointing	A	574
Spiritual Gifts And The Holy Spirit	A	605
I Will Pour Out My Spirit On All Flesh	A	625
The God Of Restoration	A	627
Deep Water	A	674
The Anointing Of The Holy Spirit	A	678
Be Filled With The Spirit	A	708

Jesus

The Spirit Of Adoption	A	592
The Good News Of Jesus	A	631
The Resurrection And The Life	A	642
The Signs Of Our Lord's Return	A	647
Christ Living In Me	A	659
There's A Lion On The Inside Of Me	A	684
Who Do You Say Jesus Is?	A	701

Prayer

Don't Stop Praying	A	628
The Praying Church	A	650
Except By Prayer And Fasting	A	661
Building An Altar	A	671
Renewing Your Mind	A	707

Single Audio Cassettes - Continued
$5.00 Each

Title	Order Number
Love	
You Are Valuable To God	A 492
God Needs You	A 493
What Would Love Do?	A 555
Searching For Love	A 577
God Loves The Backslider	A 668
Growing Up In Love	A 681
Praise And Worship	
Shout Your Way To Victory	A 477
Don't Let The Enemy Steal Your Joy	A 520
True Praise And Worship	A 595
Touching God Through Music	A 621
Having Joy In The Midst Of Trouble	A 640
Prophecy	
The Church Is A Place Of Warfare	A 636
Armed And Dangerous	A 656
A New World Order	A 666
Warfare Always Precedes A Miracle	A 667
Having Confidence In Your Future	A 691
Salvation	
The Resurrection And The Life	A 642
Crossroads	A 655
Getting Ready For The Journey	A 664
God Loves The Backslider	A 668
The Heavenly City	A 680
Let The Church Be The Church	A 706
Warfare	
No Weapon Formed Against You Shall Prosper	A 572
The Church Is A Place Of Warfare	A 636
Armed And Dangerous	A 656
Warfare Always Precedes A Miracle	A 667
Stake Your Claim	A 692
Let My People Go	A 693
The "Classics"	
World Changers And People Lifters	A 468
Grace Upon Grace	A 507
Finding Happiness	A 514
Lust, Sex And Love	A 515
Why Can't You Be Normal And Serve God	A 532
Heaven Or Hell	A 557
Character And Integrity Part 1	A 558
Which Sin Is Worse	A 561
Character And Integrity Part 2	A 564
Obey God And Live	A 596
The Blessing Or The Curse	A 602
Goals And Dreams	A 609
Living On The Edge	A 629
I'm Never Looking Back	A 676
Sexual Fulfillment	A 697

Order Form

Name

Address

City   State   Zip

Item	Title	Quantity	Amount

☐ *Check*   ☐ *Money Order*
☐ *VISA*   ☐ *Master Card*

Total Order
Contribution
Total

Expiration Date: _____
Signature: _____
Telephone Number: _____

Heritage Christian Center   9495 East Florida Avenue
Denver, Colorado 80231
(303) 369-8514